STAYING
ON THE MARK
WITH MY FITNESS GOALS

———— Fitness Journal Tracker ————

ACTIVINOTES

DAILY JOURNALS, PLANNERS, NOTEBOOKS AND OTHER BLANK BOOKS

DAILY FOOD INTAKE & FITNESS ROUTINE

BREAKFAST

TIME:

DESCRIPTION:

PROTEIN	CARBS	FATS	FRUITS / VEGGIES	CALORIES

SNACK

TIME:

DESCRIPTION:

PROTEIN	CARBS	FATS	FRUITS / VEGGIES	CALORIES

LUNCH

TIME:

DESCRIPTION:

PROTEIN	CARBS	FATS	FRUITS / VEGGIES	CALORIES

SNACK

DESCRIPTION:

PROTEIN	CARBS	FATS	FRUITS / VEGGIES	CALORIES

DINNER

TIME:

DESCRIPTION:

PROTEIN	CARBS	FATS	FRUITS / VEGGIES	CALORIES

TODAYS WORKOUT

TIME:

EXERCISE	SETS	REPS	WEIGHT	REST	NOTE

DAILY FOOD INTAKE & FITNESS ROUTINE

BREAKFAST
TIME:

DESCRIPTION:
_____
_____
_____
_____
_____

PROTEIN	CARBS	FATS	FRUITS / VEGGIES	CALORIES

SNACK
TIME:

DESCRIPTION:
_____
_____
_____

PROTEIN	CARBS	FATS	FRUITS / VEGGIES	CALORIES

LUNCH
TIME:

DESCRIPTION:
_____
_____
_____
_____

PROTEIN	CARBS	FATS	FRUITS / VEGGIES	CALORIES

SNACK

TIME:

DESCRIPTION:

PROTEIN	CARBS	FATS	FRUITS / VEGGIES	CALORIES

DINNER

TIME:

DESCRIPTION:

PROTEIN	CARBS	FATS	FRUITS / VEGGIES	CALORIES

TODAYS WORKOUT

TIME:

EXERCISE	SETS	REPS	WEIGHT	REST	NOTE

DAILY FOOD INTAKE & FITNESS ROUTINE

BREAKFAST

TIME:

DESCRIPTION:

PROTEIN	CARBS	FATS	FRUITS / VEGGIES	CALORIES

SNACK

TIME:

DESCRIPTION:

PROTEIN	CARBS	FATS	FRUITS / VEGGIES	CALORIES

LUNCH

TIME:

DESCRIPTION:

PROTEIN	CARBS	FATS	FRUITS / VEGGIES	CALORIES

SNACK

DESCRIPTION:

PROTEIN	CARBS	FATS	FRUITS / VEGGIES	CALORIES

DINNER

TIME:

DESCRIPTION:

PROTEIN	CARBS	FATS	FRUITS / VEGGIES	CALORIES

TODAYS WORKOUT

TIME:

EXERCISE	SETS	REPS	WEIGHT	REST	NOTE

DAILY FOOD INTAKE & FITNESS ROUTINE

BREAKFAST

TIME:

DESCRIPTION:

PROTEIN	CARBS	FATS	FRUITS / VEGGIES	CALORIES

SNACK

TIME:

DESCRIPTION:

PROTEIN	CARBS	FATS	FRUITS / VEGGIES	CALORIES

LUNCH

TIME:

DESCRIPTION:

PROTEIN	CARBS	FATS	FRUITS / VEGGIES	CALORIES

SNACK

TIME:

DESCRIPTION:

PROTEIN	CARBS	FATS	FRUITS / VEGGIES	CALORIES

DINNER

TIME:

DESCRIPTION:

PROTEIN	CARBS	FATS	FRUITS / VEGGIES	CALORIES

TODAYS WORKOUT

TIME:

EXERCISE	SETS	REPS	WEIGHT	REST	NOTE

DAILY FOOD INTAKE & FITNESS ROUTINE

BREAKFAST

TIME:

DESCRIPTION:

PROTEIN	CARBS	FATS	FRUITS / VEGGIES	CALORIES

SNACK

TIME:

DESCRIPTION:

PROTEIN	CARBS	FATS	FRUITS / VEGGIES	CALORIES

LUNCH

TIME:

DESCRIPTION:

PROTEIN	CARBS	FATS	FRUITS / VEGGIES	CALORIES

SNACK

DESCRIPTION:

PROTEIN	CARBS	FATS	FRUITS / VEGGIES	CALORIES

DINNER

TIME:

DESCRIPTION:

PROTEIN	CARBS	FATS	FRUITS / VEGGIES	CALORIES

TODAYS WORKOUT

TIME:

EXERCISE	SETS	REPS	WEIGHT	REST	NOTE

DAILY FOOD INTAKE & FITNESS ROUTINE

BREAKFAST

TIME:

DESCRIPTION:

PROTEIN	CARBS	FATS	FRUITS / VEGGIES	CALORIES

SNACK

TIME:

DESCRIPTION:

PROTEIN	CARBS	FATS	FRUITS / VEGGIES	CALORIES

LUNCH

TIME:

DESCRIPTION:

PROTEIN	CARBS	FATS	FRUITS / VEGGIES	CALORIES

SNACK

DESCRIPTION:

PROTEIN	CARBS	FATS	FRUITS / VEGGIES	CALORIES

DINNER

TIME:

DESCRIPTION:

PROTEIN	CARBS	FATS	FRUITS / VEGGIES	CALORIES

TODAYS WORKOUT

TIME:

EXERCISE	SETS	REPS	WEIGHT	REST	NOTE

DAILY FOOD INTAKE & FITNESS ROUTINE

BREAKFAST

TIME:

DESCRIPTION:

PROTEIN	CARBS	FATS	FRUITS / VEGGIES	CALORIES

SNACK

TIME:

DESCRIPTION:

PROTEIN	CARBS	FATS	FRUITS / VEGGIES	CALORIES

LUNCH

TIME:

DESCRIPTION:

PROTEIN	CARBS	FATS	FRUITS / VEGGIES	CALORIES

SNACK

TIME:

DESCRIPTION:

PROTEIN	CARBS	FATS	FRUITS / VEGGIES	CALORIES

DINNER

TIME:

DESCRIPTION:

PROTEIN	CARBS	FATS	FRUITS / VEGGIES	CALORIES

TODAYS WORKOUT

TIME:

EXERCISE	SETS	REPS	WEIGHT	REST	NOTE

DAILY FOOD INTAKE & FITNESS ROUTINE

BREAKFAST

TIME:

DESCRIPTION:

PROTEIN	CARBS	FATS	FRUITS / VEGGIES	CALORIES

SNACK

TIME:

DESCRIPTION:

PROTEIN	CARBS	FATS	FRUITS / VEGGIES	CALORIES

LUNCH

TIME:

DESCRIPTION:

PROTEIN	CARBS	FATS	FRUITS / VEGGIES	CALORIES

SNACK

DESCRIPTION: _____

_____

_____

_____

PROTEIN	CARBS	FATS	FRUITS / VEGGIES	CALORIES

DINNER

TIME:

DESCRIPTION: _____

_____

_____

_____

_____

PROTEIN	CARBS	FATS	FRUITS / VEGGIES	CALORIES

TODAYS WORKOUT

TIME:

EXERCISE	SETS	REPS	WEIGHT	REST	NOTE

DAILY FOOD INTAKE & FITNESS ROUTINE

BREAKFAST

TIME:

DESCRIPTION:

PROTEIN	CARBS	FATS	FRUITS / VEGGIES	CALORIES

SNACK

TIME:

DESCRIPTION:

PROTEIN	CARBS	FATS	FRUITS / VEGGIES	CALORIES

LUNCH

TIME:

DESCRIPTION:

PROTEIN	CARBS	FATS	FRUITS / VEGGIES	CALORIES

SNACK

DESCRIPTION:

PROTEIN	CARBS	FATS	FRUITS / VEGGIES	CALORIES

DINNER

TIME:

DESCRIPTION:

PROTEIN	CARBS	FATS	FRUITS / VEGGIES	CALORIES

TODAYS WORKOUT

TIME:

EXERCISE	SETS	REPS	WEIGHT	REST	NOTE

DAILY FOOD INTAKE & FITNESS ROUTINE

BREAKFAST

TIME:

DESCRIPTION:

PROTEIN	CARBS	FATS	FRUITS / VEGGIES	CALORIES

SNACK

TIME:

DESCRIPTION:

PROTEIN	CARBS	FATS	FRUITS / VEGGIES	CALORIES

LUNCH

TIME:

DESCRIPTION:

PROTEIN	CARBS	FATS	FRUITS / VEGGIES	CALORIES

SNACK

DESCRIPTION:

PROTEIN	CARBS	FATS	FRUITS / VEGGIES	CALORIES

DINNER

TIME:

DESCRIPTION:

PROTEIN	CARBS	FATS	FRUITS / VEGGIES	CALORIES

TODAYS WORKOUT

TIME:

EXERCISE	SETS	REPS	WEIGHT	REST	NOTE

DAILY FOOD INTAKE & FITNESS ROUTINE

BREAKFAST

TIME:

DESCRIPTION:

PROTEIN	CARBS	FATS	FRUITS / VEGGIES	CALORIES

SNACK

TIME:

DESCRIPTION:

PROTEIN	CARBS	FATS	FRUITS / VEGGIES	CALORIES

LUNCH

TIME:

DESCRIPTION:

PROTEIN	CARBS	FATS	FRUITS / VEGGIES	CALORIES

SNACK

DESCRIPTION:

PROTEIN	CARBS	FATS	FRUITS / VEGGIES	CALORIES

DINNER

TIME:

DESCRIPTION:

PROTEIN	CARBS	FATS	FRUITS / VEGGIES	CALORIES

TODAYS WORKOUT

TIME:

EXERCISE	SETS	REPS	WEIGHT	REST	NOTE

DAILY FOOD INTAKE & FITNESS ROUTINE

BREAKFAST

TIME:

DESCRIPTION:

PROTEIN	CARBS	FATS	FRUITS/VEGGIES	CALORIES

SNACK

TIME:

DESCRIPTION:

PROTEIN	CARBS	FATS	FRUITS/VEGGIES	CALORIES

LUNCH

TIME:

DESCRIPTION:

PROTEIN	CARBS	FATS	FRUITS/VEGGIES	CALORIES

SNACK

DESCRIPTION:

PROTEIN	CARBS	FATS	FRUITS / VEGGIES	CALORIES

DINNER

TIME:

DESCRIPTION:

PROTEIN	CARBS	FATS	FRUITS / VEGGIES	CALORIES

TODAYS WORKOUT

TIME:

EXERCISE	SETS	REPS	WEIGHT	REST	NOTE

DAILY FOOD INTAKE & FITNESS ROUTINE

BREAKFAST

TIME:

DESCRIPTION:

PROTEIN	CARBS	FATS	FRUITS / VEGGIES	CALORIES

SNACK

TIME:

DESCRIPTION:

PROTEIN	CARBS	FATS	FRUITS / VEGGIES	CALORIES

LUNCH

TIME:

DESCRIPTION:

PROTEIN	CARBS	FATS	FRUITS / VEGGIES	CALORIES

SNACK

DESCRIPTION:

PROTEIN	CARBS	FATS	FRUITS / VEGGIES	CALORIES

DINNER

TIME:

DESCRIPTION:

PROTEIN	CARBS	FATS	FRUITS / VEGGIES	CALORIES

TODAYS WORKOUT

TIME:

EXERCISE	SETS	REPS	WEIGHT	REST	NOTE

DAILY FOOD INTAKE & FITNESS ROUTINE

BREAKFAST

TIME:

DESCRIPTION:

PROTEIN	CARBS	FATS	FRUITS / VEGGIES	CALORIES

SNACK

TIME:

DESCRIPTION:

PROTEIN	CARBS	FATS	FRUITS / VEGGIES	CALORIES

LUNCH

TIME:

DESCRIPTION:

PROTEIN	CARBS	FATS	FRUITS / VEGGIES	CALORIES

SNACK

DESCRIPTION:

PROTEIN	CARBS	FATS	FRUITS / VEGGIES	CALORIES

DINNER

TIME:

DESCRIPTION:

PROTEIN	CARBS	FATS	FRUITS / VEGGIES	CALORIES

TODAYS WORKOUT

TIME:

EXERCISE	SETS	REPS	WEIGHT	REST	NOTE

DAILY FOOD INTAKE & FITNESS ROUTINE

BREAKFAST

TIME:

DESCRIPTION:

PROTEIN	CARBS	FATS	FRUITS/VEGGIES	CALORIES

SNACK

TIME:

DESCRIPTION:

PROTEIN	CARBS	FATS	FRUITS/VEGGIES	CALORIES

LUNCH

TIME:

DESCRIPTION:

PROTEIN	CARBS	FATS	FRUITS/VEGGIES	CALORIES

SNACK

DESCRIPTION:

PROTEIN	CARBS	FATS	FRUITS / VEGGIES	CALORIES

DINNER

TIME:

DESCRIPTION:

PROTEIN	CARBS	FATS	FRUITS / VEGGIES	CALORIES

TODAYS WORKOUT

TIME:

EXERCISE	SETS	REPS	WEIGHT	REST	NOTE

DAILY FOOD INTAKE & FITNESS ROUTINE

BREAKFAST

TIME:

DESCRIPTION:

PROTEIN	CARBS	FATS	FRUITS / VEGGIES	CALORIES

SNACK

TIME:

DESCRIPTION:

PROTEIN	CARBS	FATS	FRUITS / VEGGIES	CALORIES

LUNCH

TIME:

DESCRIPTION:

PROTEIN	CARBS	FATS	FRUITS / VEGGIES	CALORIES

SNACK

DESCRIPTION:

PROTEIN	CARBS	FATS	FRUITS / VEGGIES	CALORIES

DINNER

TIME:

DESCRIPTION:

PROTEIN	CARBS	FATS	FRUITS / VEGGIES	CALORIES

TODAYS WORKOUT

TIME:

EXERCISE	SETS	REPS	WEIGHT	REST	NOTE

DAILY FOOD INTAKE & FITNESS ROUTINE

BREAKFAST

TIME:

DESCRIPTION:

PROTEIN	CARBS	FATS	FRUITS / VEGGIES	CALORIES

SNACK

TIME:

DESCRIPTION:

PROTEIN	CARBS	FATS	FRUITS / VEGGIES	CALORIES

LUNCH

TIME:

DESCRIPTION:

PROTEIN	CARBS	FATS	FRUITS / VEGGIES	CALORIES

SNACK

DESCRIPTION:

_____

_____

_____

PROTEIN	CARBS	FATS	FRUITS / VEGGIES	CALORIES

DINNER

TIME:

DESCRIPTION:

_____

_____

_____

_____

_____

PROTEIN	CARBS	FATS	FRUITS / VEGGIES	CALORIES

TODAYS WORKOUT

TIME:

EXERCISE	SETS	REPS	WEIGHT	REST	NOTE

DAILY FOOD INTAKE & FITNESS ROUTINE

BREAKFAST

TIME:

DESCRIPTION:

PROTEIN	CARBS	FATS	FRUITS/VEGGIES	CALORIES

SNACK

TIME:

DESCRIPTION:

PROTEIN	CARBS	FATS	FRUITS/VEGGIES	CALORIES

LUNCH

TIME:

DESCRIPTION:

PROTEIN	CARBS	FATS	FRUITS/VEGGIES	CALORIES

SNACK

DESCRIPTION:

PROTEIN	CARBS	FATS	FRUITS / VEGGIES	CALORIES

DINNER

TIME:

DESCRIPTION:

PROTEIN	CARBS	FATS	FRUITS / VEGGIES	CALORIES

TODAYS WORKOUT

TIME:

EXERCISE	SETS	REPS	WEIGHT	REST	NOTE

DAILY FOOD INTAKE & FITNESS ROUTINE

BREAKFAST

TIME:

DESCRIPTION:

PROTEIN	CARBS	FATS	FRUITS/VEGGIES	CALORIES

SNACK

TIME:

DESCRIPTION:

PROTEIN	CARBS	FATS	FRUITS/VEGGIES	CALORIES

LUNCH

TIME:

DESCRIPTION:

PROTEIN	CARBS	FATS	FRUITS/VEGGIES	CALORIES

SNACK

TIME:

DESCRIPTION:

PROTEIN	CARBS	FATS	FRUITS / VEGGIES	CALORIES

DINNER

TIME:

DESCRIPTION:

PROTEIN	CARBS	FATS	FRUITS / VEGGIES	CALORIES

TODAYS WORKOUT

TIME:

EXERCISE	SETS	REPS	WEIGHT	REST	NOTE

DAILY FOOD INTAKE & FITNESS ROUTINE

BREAKFAST

TIME:

DESCRIPTION:

PROTEIN	CARBS	FATS	FRUITS / VEGGIES	CALORIES

SNACK

TIME:

DESCRIPTION:

PROTEIN	CARBS	FATS	FRUITS / VEGGIES	CALORIES

LUNCH

TIME:

DESCRIPTION:

PROTEIN	CARBS	FATS	FRUITS / VEGGIES	CALORIES

SNACK

DESCRIPTION:

PROTEIN	CARBS	FATS	FRUITS / VEGGIES	CALORIES

DINNER

TIME:

DESCRIPTION:

PROTEIN	CARBS	FATS	FRUITS / VEGGIES	CALORIES

TODAYS WORKOUT

TIME:

EXERCISE	SETS	REPS	WEIGHT	REST	NOTE

DAILY FOOD INTAKE & FITNESS ROUTINE

BREAKFAST

TIME:

DESCRIPTION:

PROTEIN	CARBS	FATS	FRUITS / VEGGIES	CALORIES

SNACK

TIME:

DESCRIPTION:

PROTEIN	CARBS	FATS	FRUITS / VEGGIES	CALORIES

LUNCH

TIME:

DESCRIPTION:

PROTEIN	CARBS	FATS	FRUITS / VEGGIES	CALORIES

SNACK

DESCRIPTION:

PROTEIN	CARBS	FATS	FRUITS / VEGGIES	CALORIES

DINNER

TIME:

DESCRIPTION:

PROTEIN	CARBS	FATS	FRUITS / VEGGIES	CALORIES

TODAYS WORKOUT

TIME:

EXERCISE	SETS	REPS	WEIGHT	REST	NOTE

DAILY FOOD INTAKE & FITNESS ROUTINE

BREAKFAST

TIME:

DESCRIPTION:

PROTEIN	CARBS	FATS	FRUITS / VEGGIES	CALORIES

SNACK

TIME:

DESCRIPTION:

PROTEIN	CARBS	FATS	FRUITS / VEGGIES	CALORIES

LUNCH

TIME:

DESCRIPTION:

PROTEIN	CARBS	FATS	FRUITS / VEGGIES	CALORIES

SNACK

DESCRIPTION:

PROTEIN	CARBS	FATS	FRUITS / VEGGIES	CALORIES

DINNER

TIME:

DESCRIPTION:

PROTEIN	CARBS	FATS	FRUITS / VEGGIES	CALORIES

TODAYS WORKOUT

TIME:

EXERCISE	SETS	REPS	WEIGHT	REST	NOTE

DAILY FOOD INTAKE & FITNESS ROUTINE

BREAKFAST
TIME:

DESCRIPTION:

PROTEIN	CARBS	FATS	FRUITS / VEGGIES	CALORIES

SNACK
TIME:

DESCRIPTION:

PROTEIN	CARBS	FATS	FRUITS / VEGGIES	CALORIES

LUNCH
TIME:

DESCRIPTION:

PROTEIN	CARBS	FATS	FRUITS / VEGGIES	CALORIES

SNACK

DESCRIPTION:

PROTEIN	CARBS	FATS	FRUITS / VEGGIES	CALORIES

DINNER

TIME:

DESCRIPTION:

PROTEIN	CARBS	FATS	FRUITS / VEGGIES	CALORIES

TODAYS WORKOUT

TIME:

EXERCISE	SETS	REPS	WEIGHT	REST	NOTE

DAILY FOOD INTAKE & FITNESS ROUTINE

BREAKFAST

TIME:

DESCRIPTION:

PROTEIN	CARBS	FATS	FRUITS / VEGGIES	CALORIES

SNACK

TIME:

DESCRIPTION:

PROTEIN	CARBS	FATS	FRUITS / VEGGIES	CALORIES

LUNCH

TIME:

DESCRIPTION:

PROTEIN	CARBS	FATS	FRUITS / VEGGIES	CALORIES

SNACK

DESCRIPTION:

PROTEIN	CARBS	FATS	FRUITS / VEGGIES	CALORIES

DINNER

TIME:

DESCRIPTION:

PROTEIN	CARBS	FATS	FRUITS / VEGGIES	CALORIES

TODAYS WORKOUT

TIME:

EXERCISE	SETS	REPS	WEIGHT	REST	NOTE

DAILY FOOD INTAKE & FITNESS ROUTINE

BREAKFAST

TIME:

DESCRIPTION:

PROTEIN	CARBS	FATS	FRUITS / VEGGIES	CALORIES

SNACK

TIME:

DESCRIPTION:

PROTEIN	CARBS	FATS	FRUITS / VEGGIES	CALORIES

LUNCH

TIME:

DESCRIPTION:

PROTEIN	CARBS	FATS	FRUITS / VEGGIES	CALORIES

SNACK

DESCRIPTION:

PROTEIN	CARBS	FATS	FRUITS / VEGGIES	CALORIES

DINNER

TIME:

DESCRIPTION:

PROTEIN	CARBS	FATS	FRUITS / VEGGIES	CALORIES

TODAYS WORKOUT

TIME:

EXERCISE	SETS	REPS	WEIGHT	REST	NOTE

DAILY FOOD INTAKE & FITNESS ROUTINE

BREAKFAST

TIME:

DESCRIPTION:

PROTEIN	CARBS	FATS	FRUITS / VEGGIES	CALORIES

SNACK

TIME:

DESCRIPTION:

PROTEIN	CARBS	FATS	FRUITS / VEGGIES	CALORIES

LUNCH

TIME:

DESCRIPTION:

PROTEIN	CARBS	FATS	FRUITS / VEGGIES	CALORIES

SNACK

DESCRIPTION:

PROTEIN	CARBS	FATS	FRUITS / VEGGIES	CALORIES

DINNER

TIME:

DESCRIPTION:

PROTEIN	CARBS	FATS	FRUITS / VEGGIES	CALORIES

TODAYS WORKOUT

TIME:

EXERCISE	SETS	REPS	WEIGHT	REST	NOTE

DAILY FOOD INTAKE & FITNESS ROUTINE

BREAKFAST

TIME:

DESCRIPTION:

PROTEIN	CARBS	FATS	FRUITS / VEGGIES	CALORIES

SNACK

TIME:

DESCRIPTION:

PROTEIN	CARBS	FATS	FRUITS / VEGGIES	CALORIES

LUNCH

TIME:

DESCRIPTION:

PROTEIN	CARBS	FATS	FRUITS / VEGGIES	CALORIES

SNACK

TIME:

DESCRIPTION:

PROTEIN	CARBS	FATS	FRUITS / VEGGIES	CALORIES

DINNER

TIME:

DESCRIPTION:

PROTEIN	CARBS	FATS	FRUITS / VEGGIES	CALORIES

TODAYS WORKOUT

TIME:

EXERCISE	SETS	REPS	WEIGHT	REST	NOTE

DAILY FOOD INTAKE & FITNESS ROUTINE

BREAKFAST

TIME:

DESCRIPTION:

PROTEIN	CARBS	FATS	FRUITS / VEGGIES	CALORIES

SNACK

TIME:

DESCRIPTION:

PROTEIN	CARBS	FATS	FRUITS / VEGGIES	CALORIES

LUNCH

TIME:

DESCRIPTION:

PROTEIN	CARBS	FATS	FRUITS / VEGGIES	CALORIES

SNACK

TIME:

DESCRIPTION:

PROTEIN	CARBS	FATS	FRUITS / VEGGIES	CALORIES

DINNER

TIME:

DESCRIPTION:

PROTEIN	CARBS	FATS	FRUITS / VEGGIES	CALORIES

TODAYS WORKOUT

TIME:

EXERCISE	SETS	REPS	WEIGHT	REST	NOTE

DAILY FOOD INTAKE & FITNESS ROUTINE

BREAKFAST

TIME:

DESCRIPTION:

PROTEIN	CARBS	FATS	FRUITS / VEGGIES	CALORIES

SNACK

TIME:

DESCRIPTION:

PROTEIN	CARBS	FATS	FRUITS / VEGGIES	CALORIES

LUNCH

TIME:

DESCRIPTION:

PROTEIN	CARBS	FATS	FRUITS / VEGGIES	CALORIES

SNACK

DESCRIPTION:

PROTEIN	CARBS	FATS	FRUITS / VEGGIES	CALORIES

DINNER

TIME:

DESCRIPTION:

PROTEIN	CARBS	FATS	FRUITS / VEGGIES	CALORIES

TODAYS WORKOUT

TIME:

EXERCISE	SETS	REPS	WEIGHT	REST	NOTE

DAILY FOOD INTAKE & FITNESS ROUTINE

BREAKFAST

TIME:

DESCRIPTION:

PROTEIN	CARBS	FATS	FRUITS / VEGGIES	CALORIES

SNACK

TIME:

DESCRIPTION:

PROTEIN	CARBS	FATS	FRUITS / VEGGIES	CALORIES

LUNCH

TIME:

DESCRIPTION:

PROTEIN	CARBS	FATS	FRUITS / VEGGIES	CALORIES

SNACK

TIME:

DESCRIPTION:
_____
_____
_____

PROTEIN	CARBS	FATS	FRUITS / VEGGIES	CALORIES

DINNER

TIME:

DESCRIPTION:
_____
_____
_____
_____
_____

PROTEIN	CARBS	FATS	FRUITS / VEGGIES	CALORIES

TODAYS WORKOUT

TIME:

EXERCISE	SETS	REPS	WEIGHT	REST	NOTE

DAILY FOOD INTAKE & FITNESS ROUTINE

BREAKFAST

TIME:

DESCRIPTION:

PROTEIN	CARBS	FATS	FRUITS / VEGGIES	CALORIES

SNACK

TIME:

DESCRIPTION:

PROTEIN	CARBS	FATS	FRUITS / VEGGIES	CALORIES

LUNCH

TIME:

DESCRIPTION:

PROTEIN	CARBS	FATS	FRUITS / VEGGIES	CALORIES

SNACK

TIME:

DESCRIPTION:

PROTEIN	CARBS	FATS	FRUITS / VEGGIES	CALORIES

DINNER

TIME:

DESCRIPTION:

PROTEIN	CARBS	FATS	FRUITS / VEGGIES	CALORIES

TODAYS WORKOUT

TIME:

EXERCISE	SETS	REPS	WEIGHT	REST	NOTE

DAILY FOOD INTAKE & FITNESS ROUTINE

BREAKFAST

TIME:

DESCRIPTION:

PROTEIN	CARBS	FATS	FRUITS / VEGGIES	CALORIES

SNACK

TIME:

DESCRIPTION:

PROTEIN	CARBS	FATS	FRUITS / VEGGIES	CALORIES

LUNCH

TIME:

DESCRIPTION:

PROTEIN	CARBS	FATS	FRUITS / VEGGIES	CALORIES

SNACK

DESCRIPTION:

PROTEIN	CARBS	FATS	FRUITS / VEGGIES	CALORIES

DINNER

TIME:

DESCRIPTION:

PROTEIN	CARBS	FATS	FRUITS / VEGGIES	CALORIES

TODAYS WORKOUT

TIME:

EXERCISE	SETS	REPS	WEIGHT	REST	NOTE

DAILY FOOD INTAKE & FITNESS ROUTINE

BREAKFAST

TIME:

DESCRIPTION:

PROTEIN	CARBS	FATS	FRUITS / VEGGIES	CALORIES

SNACK

TIME:

DESCRIPTION:

PROTEIN	CARBS	FATS	FRUITS / VEGGIES	CALORIES

LUNCH

TIME:

DESCRIPTION:

PROTEIN	CARBS	FATS	FRUITS / VEGGIES	CALORIES

SNACK

DESCRIPTION:

PROTEIN	CARBS	FATS	FRUITS / VEGGIES	CALORIES

DINNER

TIME:

DESCRIPTION:

PROTEIN	CARBS	FATS	FRUITS / VEGGIES	CALORIES

TODAYS WORKOUT

TIME:

EXERCISE	SETS	REPS	WEIGHT	REST	NOTE

DAILY FOOD INTAKE & FITNESS ROUTINE

BREAKFAST

TIME:

DESCRIPTION:

PROTEIN	CARBS	FATS	FRUITS / VEGGIES	CALORIES

SNACK

TIME:

DESCRIPTION:

PROTEIN	CARBS	FATS	FRUITS / VEGGIES	CALORIES

LUNCH

TIME:

DESCRIPTION:

PROTEIN	CARBS	FATS	FRUITS / VEGGIES	CALORIES

SNACK

DESCRIPTION:

PROTEIN	CARBS	FATS	FRUITS / VEGGIES	CALORIES

DINNER

TIME:

DESCRIPTION:

PROTEIN	CARBS	FATS	FRUITS / VEGGIES	CALORIES

TODAYS WORKOUT

TIME:

EXERCISE	SETS	REPS	WEIGHT	REST	NOTE

DAILY FOOD INTAKE & FITNESS ROUTINE

BREAKFAST

TIME:

DESCRIPTION:

PROTEIN	CARBS	FATS	FRUITS / VEGGIES	CALORIES

SNACK

TIME:

DESCRIPTION:

PROTEIN	CARBS	FATS	FRUITS / VEGGIES	CALORIES

LUNCH

TIME:

DESCRIPTION:

PROTEIN	CARBS	FATS	FRUITS / VEGGIES	CALORIES

SNACK

DESCRIPTION:

PROTEIN	CARBS	FATS	FRUITS / VEGGIES	CALORIES

DINNER

TIME:

DESCRIPTION:

PROTEIN	CARBS	FATS	FRUITS / VEGGIES	CALORIES

TODAYS WORKOUT

TIME:

EXERCISE	SETS	REPS	WEIGHT	REST	NOTE

DAILY FOOD INTAKE & FITNESS ROUTINE

BREAKFAST

TIME:

DESCRIPTION:

PROTEIN	CARBS	FATS	FRUITS / VEGGIES	CALORIES

SNACK

TIME:

DESCRIPTION:

PROTEIN	CARBS	FATS	FRUITS / VEGGIES	CALORIES

LUNCH

TIME:

DESCRIPTION:

PROTEIN	CARBS	FATS	FRUITS / VEGGIES	CALORIES

SNACK

TIME:

DESCRIPTION:

PROTEIN	CARBS	FATS	FRUITS / VEGGIES	CALORIES

DINNER

TIME:

DESCRIPTION:

PROTEIN	CARBS	FATS	FRUITS / VEGGIES	CALORIES

TODAYS WORKOUT

TIME:

EXERCISE	SETS	REPS	WEIGHT	REST	NOTE

DAILY FOOD INTAKE & FITNESS ROUTINE

BREAKFAST

TIME:

DESCRIPTION:

PROTEIN	CARBS	FATS	FRUITS / VEGGIES	CALORIES

SNACK

TIME:

DESCRIPTION:

PROTEIN	CARBS	FATS	FRUITS / VEGGIES	CALORIES

LUNCH

TIME:

DESCRIPTION:

PROTEIN	CARBS	FATS	FRUITS / VEGGIES	CALORIES

SNACK

TIME:

DESCRIPTION:

PROTEIN	CARBS	FATS	FRUITS / VEGGIES	CALORIES

DINNER

TIME:

DESCRIPTION:

PROTEIN	CARBS	FATS	FRUITS / VEGGIES	CALORIES

TODAYS WORKOUT

TIME:

EXERCISE	SETS	REPS	WEIGHT	REST	NOTE

DAILY FOOD INTAKE & FITNESS ROUTINE

BREAKFAST

TIME:

DESCRIPTION:

PROTEIN	CARBS	FATS	FRUITS / VEGGIES	CALORIES

SNACK

TIME:

DESCRIPTION:

PROTEIN	CARBS	FATS	FRUITS / VEGGIES	CALORIES

LUNCH

TIME:

DESCRIPTION:

PROTEIN	CARBS	FATS	FRUITS / VEGGIES	CALORIES

SNACK

DESCRIPTION:

PROTEIN	CARBS	FATS	FRUITS / VEGGIES	CALORIES

DINNER

TIME:

DESCRIPTION:

PROTEIN	CARBS	FATS	FRUITS / VEGGIES	CALORIES

TODAYS WORKOUT

TIME:

EXERCISE	SETS	REPS	WEIGHT	REST	NOTE

DAILY FOOD INTAKE & FITNESS ROUTINE

BREAKFAST

TIME:

DESCRIPTION:

PROTEIN	CARBS	FATS	FRUITS / VEGGIES	CALORIES

SNACK

TIME:

DESCRIPTION:

PROTEIN	CARBS	FATS	FRUITS / VEGGIES	CALORIES

LUNCH

TIME:

DESCRIPTION:

PROTEIN	CARBS	FATS	FRUITS / VEGGIES	CALORIES

SNACK

DESCRIPTION:
_____
_____
_____

PROTEIN	CARBS	FATS	FRUITS / VEGGIES	CALORIES

DINNER

TIME:

DESCRIPTION:
_____
_____
_____
_____
_____

PROTEIN	CARBS	FATS	FRUITS / VEGGIES	CALORIES

TODAYS WORKOUT

TIME:

EXERCISE	SETS	REPS	WEIGHT	REST	NOTE

DAILY FOOD INTAKE & FITNESS ROUTINE

BREAKFAST

TIME:

DESCRIPTION:

PROTEIN	CARBS	FATS	FRUITS / VEGGIES	CALORIES

SNACK

TIME:

DESCRIPTION:

PROTEIN	CARBS	FATS	FRUITS / VEGGIES	CALORIES

LUNCH

TIME:

DESCRIPTION:

PROTEIN	CARBS	FATS	FRUITS / VEGGIES	CALORIES

SNACK

DESCRIPTION:

PROTEIN	CARBS	FATS	FRUITS / VEGGIES	CALORIES

DINNER

TIME:

DESCRIPTION:

PROTEIN	CARBS	FATS	FRUITS / VEGGIES	CALORIES

TODAYS WORKOUT

TIME:

EXERCISE	SETS	REPS	WEIGHT	REST	NOTE

DAILY FOOD INTAKE & FITNESS ROUTINE

BREAKFAST

TIME:

DESCRIPTION:

PROTEIN	CARBS	FATS	FRUITS / VEGGIES	CALORIES

SNACK

TIME:

DESCRIPTION:

PROTEIN	CARBS	FATS	FRUITS / VEGGIES	CALORIES

LUNCH

TIME:

DESCRIPTION:

PROTEIN	CARBS	FATS	FRUITS / VEGGIES	CALORIES

SNACK

DESCRIPTION:

PROTEIN	CARBS	FATS	FRUITS / VEGGIES	CALORIES

DINNER

TIME:

DESCRIPTION:

PROTEIN	CARBS	FATS	FRUITS / VEGGIES	CALORIES

TODAYS WORKOUT

TIME:

EXERCISE	SETS	REPS	WEIGHT	REST	NOTE

DAILY FOOD INTAKE & FITNESS ROUTINE

BREAKFAST

TIME:

DESCRIPTION:

PROTEIN	CARBS	FATS	FRUITS / VEGGIES	CALORIES

SNACK

TIME:

DESCRIPTION:

PROTEIN	CARBS	FATS	FRUITS / VEGGIES	CALORIES

LUNCH

TIME:

DESCRIPTION:

PROTEIN	CARBS	FATS	FRUITS / VEGGIES	CALORIES

SNACK

TIME:

DESCRIPTION:

PROTEIN	CARBS	FATS	FRUITS / VEGGIES	CALORIES

DINNER

TIME:

DESCRIPTION:

PROTEIN	CARBS	FATS	FRUITS / VEGGIES	CALORIES

TODAYS WORKOUT

TIME:

EXERCISE	SETS	REPS	WEIGHT	REST	NOTE

DAILY FOOD INTAKE & FITNESS ROUTINE

BREAKFAST

TIME:

DESCRIPTION:

PROTEIN	CARBS	FATS	FRUITS / VEGGIES	CALORIES

SNACK

TIME:

DESCRIPTION:

PROTEIN	CARBS	FATS	FRUITS / VEGGIES	CALORIES

LUNCH

TIME:

DESCRIPTION:

PROTEIN	CARBS	FATS	FRUITS / VEGGIES	CALORIES

SNACK

DESCRIPTION:

PROTEIN	CARBS	FATS	FRUITS / VEGGIES	CALORIES

DINNER

TIME:

DESCRIPTION:

PROTEIN	CARBS	FATS	FRUITS / VEGGIES	CALORIES

TODAYS WORKOUT

TIME:

EXERCISE	SETS	REPS	WEIGHT	REST	NOTE

DAILY FOOD INTAKE & FITNESS ROUTINE

BREAKFAST

TIME:

DESCRIPTION:

PROTEIN	CARBS	FATS	FRUITS / VEGGIES	CALORIES

SNACK

TIME:

DESCRIPTION:

PROTEIN	CARBS	FATS	FRUITS / VEGGIES	CALORIES

LUNCH

TIME:

DESCRIPTION:

PROTEIN	CARBS	FATS	FRUITS / VEGGIES	CALORIES

SNACK

DESCRIPTION:
_____
_____
_____

PROTEIN	CARBS	FATS	FRUITS / VEGGIES	CALORIES

DINNER

TIME:

DESCRIPTION:
_____
_____
_____
_____
_____

PROTEIN	CARBS	FATS	FRUITS / VEGGIES	CALORIES

TODAYS WORKOUT

TIME:

EXERCISE	SETS	REPS	WEIGHT	REST	NOTE

DAILY FOOD INTAKE & FITNESS ROUTINE

BREAKFAST

TIME:

DESCRIPTION:

PROTEIN	CARBS	FATS	FRUITS / VEGGIES	CALORIES

SNACK

TIME:

DESCRIPTION:

PROTEIN	CARBS	FATS	FRUITS / VEGGIES	CALORIES

LUNCH

TIME:

DESCRIPTION:

PROTEIN	CARBS	FATS	FRUITS / VEGGIES	CALORIES

SNACK

DESCRIPTION:

PROTEIN	CARBS	FATS	FRUITS / VEGGIES	CALORIES

DINNER

DESCRIPTION:

PROTEIN	CARBS	FATS	FRUITS / VEGGIES	CALORIES

TODAYS WORKOUT

EXERCISE	SETS	REPS	WEIGHT	REST	NOTE

DAILY FOOD INTAKE & FITNESS ROUTINE

BREAKFAST

TIME:

DESCRIPTION:

PROTEIN	CARBS	FATS	FRUITS / VEGGIES	CALORIES

SNACK

TIME:

DESCRIPTION:

PROTEIN	CARBS	FATS	FRUITS / VEGGIES	CALORIES

LUNCH

TIME:

DESCRIPTION:

PROTEIN	CARBS	FATS	FRUITS / VEGGIES	CALORIES

SNACK

DESCRIPTION:

PROTEIN	CARBS	FATS	FRUITS / VEGGIES	CALORIES

DINNER

DESCRIPTION:

PROTEIN	CARBS	FATS	FRUITS / VEGGIES	CALORIES

TODAYS WORKOUT

EXERCISE	SETS	REPS	WEIGHT	REST	NOTE

DAILY FOOD INTAKE & FITNESS ROUTINE

BREAKFAST

TIME:

DESCRIPTION:

PROTEIN	CARBS	FATS	FRUITS / VEGGIES	CALORIES

SNACK

TIME:

DESCRIPTION:

PROTEIN	CARBS	FATS	FRUITS / VEGGIES	CALORIES

LUNCH

TIME:

DESCRIPTION:

PROTEIN	CARBS	FATS	FRUITS / VEGGIES	CALORIES

SNACK

DESCRIPTION:

PROTEIN	CARBS	FATS	FRUITS / VEGGIES	CALORIES

DINNER

TIME:

DESCRIPTION:

PROTEIN	CARBS	FATS	FRUITS / VEGGIES	CALORIES

TODAYS WORKOUT

TIME:

EXERCISE	SETS	REPS	WEIGHT	REST	NOTE

DAILY FOOD INTAKE & FITNESS ROUTINE

BREAKFAST

TIME:

DESCRIPTION:

PROTEIN	CARBS	FATS	FRUITS / VEGGIES	CALORIES

SNACK

TIME:

DESCRIPTION:

PROTEIN	CARBS	FATS	FRUITS / VEGGIES	CALORIES

LUNCH

TIME:

DESCRIPTION:

PROTEIN	CARBS	FATS	FRUITS / VEGGIES	CALORIES

SNACK

DESCRIPTION:

PROTEIN	CARBS	FATS	FRUITS / VEGGIES	CALORIES

DINNER

TIME:

DESCRIPTION:

PROTEIN	CARBS	FATS	FRUITS / VEGGIES	CALORIES

TODAYS WORKOUT

TIME:

EXERCISE	SETS	REPS	WEIGHT	REST	NOTE

DAILY FOOD INTAKE & FITNESS ROUTINE

BREAKFAST

TIME:

DESCRIPTION:

PROTEIN	CARBS	FATS	FRUITS / VEGGIES	CALORIES

SNACK

TIME:

DESCRIPTION:

PROTEIN	CARBS	FATS	FRUITS / VEGGIES	CALORIES

LUNCH

TIME:

DESCRIPTION:

PROTEIN	CARBS	FATS	FRUITS / VEGGIES	CALORIES

SNACK

DESCRIPTION:

PROTEIN	CARBS	FATS	FRUITS / VEGGIES	CALORIES

DINNER

TIME:

DESCRIPTION:

PROTEIN	CARBS	FATS	FRUITS / VEGGIES	CALORIES

TODAYS WORKOUT

TIME:

EXERCISE	SETS	REPS	WEIGHT	REST	NOTE